Happer's

Grammar

Boot Camp

Richard Happer

JonesCat
PUBLISHING

Published by JonesCat Publishing Ltd
Edinburgh EH10 4LW

Copyright © Richard Happer 2015

ISBN 9780956242846 – eBook
ISBN 9780956242853 – print

This book is dedicated to my father, Mark, for sending me to the dictionary every single sodding time I wanted to know what a word meant. Then, I was furious and wished with a red heat in my chest that you would just bloody tell me. But now, 30 years later, I see what you were up to.

And I thank you.

Richardxxx

'I have spent most of the day putting in a comma and the rest of the day taking it out.'

Oscar Wilde

'My spelling is Wobbly. It's good spelling but it Wobbles, and the letters get in the wrong places.'

Winnie-the-Pooh

INTRODUCTION

You can write beautiful English. I guarantee it.

That or which? Where does the apostrophe go? What is an infinitive, and why do people get so wound up about splitting it?

Oh man, not another grammar know-it-all banging on about petty rules that are only designed to trip me up and make him feel clever and that don't matter anyway and-

Woah, dragon!

'Ways of writing English that have proven to be the most clear and expressive.'

That's my definition of grammar. Noam Chomsky probably has a different one. So does Eminem. So what? I understand them both.

Even the experts don't agree on everything. But there are very widely accepted standards on most elements of writing, including how to write clear business English.

On the one hand, it's good that we have these accepted ways of writing well. They can help you express yourself perfectly. That can be very useful. Many employers use CVs with spelling mistakes as paper aeroplanes. These employers want to create a company that values quality. They know their customers care about details. So they want employees who can make a good impression and focus on the details. Because then they'll make lots of cash.

On the other hand, many of these rules are bonkers. They hinder clear and graceful writing. The best writers have been ignoring them for centuries.

For example, the whole split infinitives brouhaha grew from the notion that English should emulate Latin. That's a crackpot idea! And why should the original meaning of a word be the only correct one? Sometimes, on closer examination, what many people assume is a never-to-be-broken rule is actually a question of style. It's not: are you right or are you wrong? It's: do you want to write informally or formally?

Sadly, to some people even the bonkers rules are traps. If you don't spot them then they will pounce and tear you apart. Yeah, I hate those people too. I call them the Grammar Trappers.

But if you spend a little time learning the tricks, then using them becomes second nature. 'Mirror, Signal, Manoeuvre' sounded baffling at first, but you don't even think about it when you get in the car now.

It's like the old sign at the swimming pool: 'No running, no bombing, no petting...' If you follow those few simple guidelines, then the lifeguard won't throw you out. You can dive in and have some fun.

It's the same thing with grammar. Get the rules in your head (or at your fingertips in a handy wee eBook) and the pool of language is yours. You can even do some petting if you know which corners to hide in…

In my Grammar Boot Camp I run you through 31 of the most common grammar topics in written English. This book is short, but it covers 99 per cent of the Wobbles that Pooh and the rest of us have when writing. I give straightforward explanations and just enough technical stuff to help it all make sense. My examples are simple and clear. Occasionally I try to be amusing (forgive me). You can spend five minutes each day reading a tip and one month later you'll have the confidence to master any sentence. They are wrong. So wrong. This little guide tells you exactly how. So you can beat the Grammar Trapper know-it-alls at their own game.

Why listen to me?

I have been a professional writer for 18 years. As a copywriter I have created advertising for brands you see every day. My finely crafted phrases have enticed you to buy stuff you probably didn't need: whisky, Guinness, Pot Noodles, personal loans. Sorry about that. But I also write nice things like books about space, novels and children's fiction.

This book began life as a series of daily emails that I sent round to all the staff of an advertising agency I worked in. That wasn't a smart-arse move; my boss asked me to. And people loved it. They requested more tips, added examples and, sometimes, corrected me. A lot of thought and experience has been distilled into these pages.

So I know for a fact that this course works. You really will get something out of it. Even if you remember one solitary tip you'll feel a little bit more confident when you next sit down to write. And if you remember a lot of things, then you'll feel positively empowered.

English is your language as much as it is anyone else's. Here is where you take control of it. Who knows then what wondrous words will come when you call?

Come on, swim with me.

Richard

TABLE OF CONTENTS

DAY 1

Are we staying in a hotel? Or an hotel?

These are questions that will ruin the weekend before you've even checked in. 'Do we get a free bottle of fizz?' is more relevant, but doesn't pose any grammatical problems.

We've all known that you say **a giraffe** but **an elephant** since we were two years old.

That's important – we learn to speak before we learn to write. It's **a** thing if the thing starts with a consonant and **an** thing if the thing starts with a vowel.

But you do have to pay attention to **a** and **an** (the indefinite articles as they are also known).

Because although **ewe** starts with an **e** when you spell it, it actually starts with the consonant **y**. It sounds like **you**.

So we say:

> A female sheep is a ewe.

Not:

> A female sheep is an ewe.

Now here are some examples you might actually come across. We write:

> A £70,000 mortgage (starts with a consonant sound)

But:

> An £80,000 mortgage (vowel sound)

Although which jammy bastard only has 80 grand on their frigging mortgage?

We write:

> A stamped, addressedenvelope(starts with a
> consonant sound, **st**)

but:

> An S.A.E. (starts with a vowel sound – in your
> head you are saying **ess-ay-ee**.

The same rule regarding sound rather than spelling applies to abbreviation:

> **a** CD but **an** LP.

In your head you are saying **see-dee** (starts with a consonant) and **ell-pee** (start with a vowel.)

And in a neat flip of the **a** rule, this is also true when an unpronounced consonant comes first: **an heir** (which sounds like it is spelt **air**).

Right, let's get back to that hotel, baby.

The reason anyone ever said an hotel is because the emphasis in the word hotel was on the second syllable:

> an ho**TEL**
> an hy**STER**ical English teacher.

Because the stress came on the second syllable, the first one was rushed and the phlegm-creating **h** sound was simply lost. It became **an oTEL**.

Not even the most strict of grammarians ever said **an hat**. A cockney might but that is a whole other can of worms.

The truth is that saying **an hotel** nowadays sounds old-fashioned to most people. It really is falling from use. BUT there are some people who think it is correct.

Which kind of person have you just run away with?

DAY 2

You're hyphen a laugh

The man eating shark

Consider the headline above. At first glance, it appears to be describing some terrifying fish. However, in reality, it's referring to a man in a restaurant enjoying a meal. The scary version requires a hyphen:

The man-eating shark

Hyphens come in very handy when you are describing things with more than one word and you want to fully clarify your meaning. Here are some more examples:

>   The pickled onion seller (a drunk onion seller
>   The pickled-onion seller (someone selling pickled
>   onions)
>
>   The light green dress (a lightweight garment)
>   The light-green dress (a garment that is light in
>   colour)
>
>   The first class meeting (first in a series of class
>   meetings)
>   The first-class meeting (a great meeting)

Sometimes, you may need to use two hyphens to connect three describing words:

the at-a-glance guide to good grammar

Also, this only applies if the compound precedes the noun:

> a well-drawn face
> her blood-red scarf
> it was a well-known fact
> a fifteenth-century manuscript
> a well-liked man

However, if the compound follows the noun then the hyphen is unnecessary:

> the face was well drawn
> her scarf was blood red
> the fact was well known
> the manuscript dates from the fifteenth century
> the man was well liked

However, do not use hyphens when the compound's first part ends in **–ly**:

> a happily married couple
> a newly discovered manuscript
> a prettily furnished room
> a highly competitive market

Does your compound look like a car crash rather than a beautiful union? Then use a hyphen:

> de-ice
> drip-proof
> non-effective

> pre-eminent
> pre-empt
> re-entry
> semi-invalid

but note:

> cooperate
> coordinate

You should also use a hyphen to yoke a prefix to a proper name:

> anti-Darwinism
> pseudo-Augustan

and to avoid confusion with a similar word:

> re-form (to distinguish from 'reform')
> re-cover (to distinguish from 'recover')
> re-sort (to distinguish from resort)

Hyphens belong in spelt-out numbers and fractions:

> thirty-three
> two-thirds

but not in compass points:

> northeast
> Southeast Asia

Until you make further compounds for the wind directions,

then you need a hyphen:

> East-southeast

Some family titles hyphenate, some do not:

> grandfather
> granddaughter
> great-aunt
> stepmother
> great-great-grandfather

DAY 3

Brackets (in parenthesis)

Brackets can seem complex, but really they're very simple. They are used to insert a word or phrase that comments on or explains part of the sentence in which it is found.

Since the basic idea is that they are used to contain an addition to the sentence, a good check to see if you're using them correctly is to ask yourself if the sentence would still make sense if you took the words in the brackets away.

Wrong:

> August in Edinburgh is wonderful (apart from the weather), that is.

Because:

> August in Edinburgh, that is.

does not form a proper sentence.

Right:

> August in Edinburgh is wonderful (apart from the weather, that is).

Because

> August in Edinburgh is wonderful.

does form a complete sentence.

Where does the full stop go?

If the sentence in the brackets is complete, it goes inside:

> Russell Brand is a political activist. (He is also a joker.)

If it is just a phrase or part of a sentence, it goes outside:

> Advertising is a business for crooks (according to my father).

Bracketed material also goes in front of commas:

> As the most devilishly handsome ginger man in Edinburgh (in his own opinion), Richard felt very confident meeting the new freelance girl.

One common mistake is to use both commas and brackets:

> As the most devilishly handsome ginger man in Edinburgh, (in his own opinion), Richard felt very confident meeting the new freelance girl.

The commas and the brackets are, in effect, doing the same job. So you don't need both of them. The first example is correct.

Finally...

Parenthesis can mean either an actual bracket '(' or ')' or a word or phrase that is within brackets or dashes. The plural of *parenthesis* is *parentheses*. Although, please note that the phrase *in parenthesis,* which refers to bracketed material, uses the singular. So:

> This is a pair of parentheses: ()
> This phrase is in parenthesis (just as an example).

Use square brackets to enclose interpolations by any third
party in quoted matter:

> He wrote to his brother to say that 'whatever
> indications to the contrary he [the Prime Minister]
> may have given, my position remains the same'.

DAY 4

Comma chameleon

Commas are like grated cheese. They look a bit like little cheese gratings, to start with. They can also be used to add flavour. But, oh boy, do people sometimes add too much.

This is understandable: cheese has many wonderful uses. Sorry, commas. But when should you use a comma?

You may have been told to use a comma when you pause in your sentence. That's a bit like saying you need to use your brake pedal when it's time to slow down. It's correct, but it misses the point somewhat. 'Why does your sentence need a pause?' is the important question.

The answer is usually that you need the comma to one of four jobs:

1. The Listing Comma
2. The Joining Comma
3. The Gapping Comma
4. The Bracketing Comma

1. The Listing Comma

a. Use a comma in an X, Y and Z list

Commas make lists of three or more items readable. They work as a replacement for the word **and** or or.

> mad, bad and dangerous to know
> The Three Musketeers were Athos, Porthos and
> Aramis.

You can separate a list of phrases with commas:

> Steve speaks Spanish, Juliet speaks Japanese and I
> speak Italian.

In a list of three or more items, you shouldn't normally add a comma before the **and** (or before **or**) in such a list. This is known as the serial or Oxford comma:

> an index of social, economic and religious diversity
> You have a choice of red, blue or green.

The exception is when leaving the Oxford comma out would make the sentence confusing:

> I'd like to dedicate this Accountant of the Year
> award to my parents, Susie Jones and Jesus.

That sounds like your mum is Susie Jones and Jesus is your dad.

> I'd like to dedicate this Accountant of the Year
> award to my parents, Susie Jones, and Jesus.

The Oxford comma is used more often in American English than in British English.

b. Use a comma to separate adjectives.

When adjectives are all referring to the same thing, you can separate them with commas:

> The tall, distinguished, good-looking Scotsman.

But we can't in:

> The little old lady.

Why not? Because in the first example all the adjectives are referring to the **Scotsman**, but in the second one **old** is referring to the **lady** and **little** is referring to **old lady**: a subtle difference.

The way to check this is that if you can put **and, but** or **or** between the adjectives, then you need a comma. So you could say:

> He is a tall and distinguished fellow.

But you wouldn't say:

> She is a little and old lady.

Here's another example. We would write:

> I prefer Australian red wines to all others.

Not:

> I prefer Australian, red wines to all others.

That's because **red** is referring to wines, but **Australian** is referring to **red wines**. The adjectives are modifying different things, so you can't separate them with a comma. Remember, to check this, see if you can write **and** instead:

> I prefer Australian and red wines to all others.

This doesn't make much sense.

You would say:

> I live in a very old and leaky tent.

so you could also say:

> I live in a very old, leaky tent.

I'd think you were crazy, but grammatically correct.

2. The Joining Comma

Do you want to link two complete sentences together? You can do this with a comma, but the golden rule is that you can't do this with ONLY a comma. Instead, you need:

> a comma and one of these joining words (or conjuntions): **and**, **or**, **but**, **while** and **yet**.

So if we have these two sentences:

> The British are hopeless at learning foreign languages. The Dutch are famously good at it.

We can never just link them with a comma:

> The British are hopeless at learning foreign
> languages, the Dutch are famously good at it.

This is called the Comma Splice and, apart from apostrophes, it is probably Punctuation Mistake Number One.

But we can easily join the two sentences if we just use a comma AND a joining word. So our example becomes:

> The British are hopeless at learning foreign
> languages, but the Dutch are famously good at it.

and another one:

> She was a fantastic kisser. She would never be as
> good as her sister.
> She was a fantastic kisser, but she would never be as
> good as her sister.

The other way you can join two sentences is with a semicolon. This does not usually need a joining word:

> The British are hopeless at learning foreign
> languages; the Dutch are famously good at it.

Watch out for the words **however, therefore, hence, consequently, nevertheless** and **thus**. They are joining words but they CAN'T be used after a joining comma. You need to use a semicolon:

> Pluto was thought to be a planet, however, this is

> now known not to be the case.

is wrong, it should be:

> Pluto was thought to be a planet; however, this is
> now known not to be the case.

You don't need a comma with the joining word **because**:

> She didn't feel hungry because she had already eaten
> two Big Macs.

Unless the **because clause** needs to be set off with a comma
in order to avoid any confusion:

> I knew she would not be hungry, because my sister
> works in McDonalds and had seen her eating a
> huge meal earlier in the day.

Take the comma out of this example and the being hungry
refers to the sister's working in a restaurant, which is not the
intended meaning.

The Joining Comma Golden Rule

But you really only have to remember one golden rule:

> To link two complete sentences use a joining
> comma and one of the words **and**, **or**, **but**, **yet** or
> **while**. Don't use a joining comma in any other way.

3. The Gapping Comma

Are you repeating a phrase twice in one sentence? Then a Gapping Comma can help. You simply take out the repetition of the phrase and plug the gap with a comma.

> Some Swedes wanted to base their national language on the speech of the capital city; others, on the speech of the rural countryside.

The comma after others is a Gapping comma. It replaces a clunky repetition of the words **wanted to base their national language**. In full this sentence would have been:

> Some Swedes wanted to base their national language on the speech of the capital city; others wanted to base it on the speech of the rural countryside.

However, if a sentence is clear without a Gapping Comma you can leave it out.

4. The Bracketing Comma

You can use commas to separate out non-essential information. That is, they are used in a bracketing manner:

> If your sentence has an **aside**, an element that could be removed without changing the overall meaning, then you can set it off with commas.

This could easily be:

> If your sentence has an **aside** then you can set it off
> with commas.

This non-essential bit is known as a weak interruption.
Usually it occurs in the middle of a sentence. Here are a few
more examples:

> Steve, the geekiest guy in California, was always
> talking about computers.

> London, once the largest city in the world, is now
> visited by 16 million people a year.

Just remember that you need two commas, one at either end
of the element that you are putting as an aside.

If the aside is closely tied to the subject, then you may not
need it.

> My girlfriend, Lucy, is the world's worst accordion
> player.

could also be:

> My girlfriend Lucy is the world's worst accordion
> player.

Bracketing phrases at the start or end

Sometimes the weak interruption can come at the beginning

of a sentence:

> All in all, I think we can say that party went well.

> Having worked for years in Italy, Jim knows a lot about pasta.

or at the end:

> Europe's biggest street parade is in Notting Hill, an area of London.

> The pass rate of A-levels is rising, we believe.

Just as when the weak interruption occurred mid-sentence, it can be omitted here and these sentences would read well.

The following common words often introduce weak interruptions containing complete sentences: although, though, even though, because, since, after, before, if, when and whenever.

> Although Chilean wines are a fairly new phenomenon, they have already established a fine reputation.

> Columbus is said to have discovered America, even though the Vikings had preceded him by several centuries.

The weak interruption can be very short, but very important. Consider this sign:

> No dogs please.

Although the shopkeeper wanted to discourage patrons from entering his premises with their pooches, he omitted an essential comma. As a result, he is actually presenting the idea that **all dogs do not please**. The sign should read:

> No dogs, please.

The single word **please** is a weak interruption; in theory it could be removed.

Is it really a weak interruption?

Sometimes a phrase that looks like a weak interruption isn't. This might look like the bracketing commas have been added correctly:

> The people of Fife, who depend upon fishing for their livelihood, are up in arms over the new EC quotas.

But if you take them away:

> The people of Fife are up in arms over the new EC quotas.

You'll see that the meaning has changed. The sentence is setting out to say that it's only the people in Fife who work in fishing who are up in arms, not everyone in the region. So the bracketed phrase here isn't a weak interruption at all, but an essential part of the sentence. It should be written without any commas at all:

The people of Fife who depend upon fishing for their livelihood are up in arms over the new EC quotas.

To summarise the rules of bracketing commas:

Use a pair of bracketing commas to set off a weak interruption. This interruption could be removed from the sentence without destroying it.

If the interruption starts or ends the sentence, use only one bracketing comma.

Make sure the words set off are really an interruption.

Other uses of the comma

To separate direct speech or quoted elements from the rest of the sentence.

We'll cover quotations fully in Day 10. However, in short, commas are used to separate direct speech or quoted elements from the rest of a sentence.

'That school there,' he whispered, 'is where I first felt fear.'

You don't need a comma if another punctuation mark is clearly separating the quoted element from the rest of the sentence.

'Give me the phone!' he yelled.

Just as you have to avoid the comma splice in ordinary writing, so you have to watch out for it in quoted text:

> 'That beer looks lovely,' he said, 'will someone please buy me one?'

The sections either side of the **he said** are separate sentences and need a full stop:

> 'That beer looks lovely,' he said. 'Will someone please buy me one?'

Don't use commas to set off quoted elements introduced by the word **that** or quoted elements that are embedded in a larger structure:

> James Steward writes that 'the purpose of Angry Birds is to increase one's skill…'

> We often say 'Thank you' when we don't really mean it.

If you are setting off a very long or formal quoted element, especially of more than one sentence, use a colon:

> Peter Smith had this to say about the use of mustard as an enema: 'This was a medical practice flawed in its very conception…'

You can use commas to separate elements in a sentence

that express contrast.

These are often signaled by the words **not**, **but** and **never**.

> She was first attracted to his charm, not his billion-dollar super-yacht.
>
> His yacht is big, but vulgar.
>
> Men like him are rich, never classy.

You can use commas as typographical markers.

This is an essential way of separating dates and years, towns and counties, cities and countries, etc.

> Her cat was neutered on March 13, 2010
>
> They all moved to Houston, Texas, in February.

Oxford/Cambridge colleges mostly take parenthetical commas:

> He went up to Trinity College, Cambridge, in 1920.

But note the preferred absence of commas for the following institutions:

> King's College Cambridge
> University College London
> Trinity College Dublin

You should also use a comma before extensions such as **etc.**, **and so forth**:

lions, tigers, cheetahs, etc.

DAY 5

A refreshing colonic procedure

Do you think the colon and semicolon are too much hassle to bother with? Think again. They are very useful and not as difficult to master as you might imagine.

In the punctuation family they are closely related, yet also distinctly different from each other. Like lemons and limes.

Colons

Use colons to mark a step forward, for example from premise to conclusion:

> Study to acquire a habit of thinking: no study is more important.

and to introduce examples:

> Always remember the ancient maxim: Know thyself.

The words that follow the colon explain the words that come before the colon. Here's an example:

> The general information goes here: the specific information, here.

> Lee really likes fruit: especially apples.

Note that the text that comes after a colon can be a full sentence or a partial sentence.

Also, if you are American, something new appears immediately after the colon: A capital letter.

Semicolons

A semicolon, on the other hand, links two closely-related full sentences together.

> Lee likes all kinds of fruit; Eleanor likes pine nuts.

> Dogs have owners; cats have staff.

So the text that comes after a semicolon has to be its own sentence. A semicolon could be replaced by a full stop:

> Dogs have owners. Cats have staff.

A colon can sometimes be replaced by a full stop, but not always.

Commas are used to separate words in a list. But when the list contains phrases of many words, you can also use semicolons to create a clear division.

> Here are the things I love about the beach: the feel of sand between my toes; the wind in my hair; the sound of the surf; and you, beside me to share each moment.

Of course, you can do very well without using semicolons at all. Especially if you are Kurt Vonnegut:

> 'Do not use semicolons. They are transvestite

hermaphrodites, representing nothing. All they do is show you've been to college.'

DAY 6

To boldly go: mending the split inifinitive

Nothing in the wonderful world of the English language gets the Grammar Trappers as irate as split infinitives. They lay down the law as holy writ: 'Thou shalt not split an infinitive'.

First of all, what the hell is an infinitive? Simply put, it is the form of a verb with **to** before it, e.g.:

> To run
> To jump
> To improve your grammar

What do we mean by splitting it? Putting an adverb or other qualifying phrase in between **to** and the verb, e.g.:

> To quickly run
> To athletically jump
> To proactively improve your grammar

The Grammar Trappers will also often insist that you do not split a verb:

> I will always love you

is wrong, they say, it should be:

> I always will love you

So are they right about this? What do you think? Correct – the answer is 'no, they are not.'

The whole issue is based a daft analogy to Latin. In that language you **cannot** split a verb because it is just one word:

amare – to love

But why should you apply that rule to English? You shouldn't. The issue is one of style and not grammar. English grammar freely separates particles, auxiliary verbs, and other devices from the words to which they belong, e.g.:

I have never been to Paris

separates **have** from **been**.

You can tie yourself, and your sentences in knots trying to unsplit infinitives. You can also make things hard for the reader.

The directors voted immediately to approve the free drinks trolley.

This is a wonderfully unsplit infinitive, but what's the meaning here? Was the vote immediate or the approval?

The directors voted to immediately approve the free drinks trolley.

is instantly clearer, but the Grammar Trappers would say it is a mistake. They are plain wrong.

Of course, you shouldn't just go about splitting infinitives willy-nilly. Sometimes your sentence will sound better if you move the adverb towards the end. Also, if your modifier is something woolly such as **really, just** or **actually**, by examining your sentence you might decide to just take it out – sorry, I'll rephrase – you might decide to take it out.

Finally, it is important to acknowledge that some people will judge you for frequently splitting infinitives in formal writing, no matter how unfounded that prejudice may be. Think of it as equivalent to going into work wearing a sheer blouse: it's not illegal and you have every right to dress how you like, but the fact is that blouse is going to make some people think you are unprofessional.

In summary

The split infinitive has a long history of use and is not a cardinal sin; it is acceptable when the rhythm and meaning of the sentence call for it or when its use is that of a set verb phrase. It should be avoided (either by repositioning or rephrasing) when it seems stilted or awkward, or especially in formal writing where its inclusion may draw criticism.

After all, which one of these sounds best?

> To go, boldly, where no man has gone before.
> To go where no man has gone before, boldly.
> To boldly go where no man has gone before.

DAY 7

Pull the stops out

There is a very simple rule for abbreviations: if the abbreviation ends with the last letter of the word being abbreviated, you don't need to include a full stop.

For example, **Mister Happer** can be shortened to **Mr Happer**. Because **Mr** contains the last letter of **Mister**, you don't need to use a full stop. Therefore, if you abbreviate **Limited** to **Ltd**, you don't need a full stop. Easy.

On the other hand if you abbreviate a word and cut it off in the middle, then you need to use a full stop. For example, you can abbreviate the word **general** to **gen.** but you need to include a full stop to signify that **n** is not the last letter of **general**.

As ever, the English language contains a couple of exceptions. The abbreviation **no.** has a full stop, even though it is short for **numero** (this is to differentiate it from **no**, the abbreviation for the radioactive element **nobelium)**. Don't ask us how they came up with that one.

Similarly, **street** is abbreviated to **st.** (with a stop), but **saint** is abbreviated to **st** (without a stop). Check a good writers' dictionary for details (or even a good writer's dictionary).

And if you're talking about your French cousin Monsieur Happer, he is always M. Happer, with a full point.

So, to recap – words shortened to the initial and final letter(s) do not require a full point:

Mr/Mrs/Ms

Mme/Mlle
Dr
St (Saint)
Revd (not Rev.)
Ltd

DAY 8

I am capabile of better spelling

Adding **able** and **ible** are very common ways of forming adjectives from verbs.

These two suffixes do the same job and sound the same. But sometimes you use one and sometimes the other one.

Sometimes you have a red wine and sometimes you have a white. They certainly both get the job done. But it does pay to know the difference.

With a few exceptions, most words ending in silent e lose the e when -able is added:

> adorable
> excusable
> immovable
> lovable
> removable
> usable

Exceptions include:

> likeable
> liveable
> saleable

The e is also retained in words ending in -ce or -ge:

noticeable
serviceable
bridgeable
changeable

Frequently used words ending in –ible, rather than –able, include:

accessible, admissible, audible
compatible, comprehensible, contemptible, credible
defensible, destructible, digestible, discernible, divisible
edible, eligible, exhaustible
fallible, feasible, forcible
implausible, inaccessible, inadmissible, incompatible, irresistible
permissible
reversible
suggestible

Time for an irresistible beer…

DAY 9

Quote unquote

You should use single quotation marks around quoted matter:

> 'I do not wish to stay here,' he said.

Then use double quotation marks for quotations within quotations:

> 'Do you know what "soixante-neuf" means?' she asked.

Use single quotation marks for titles of short poems, individual cantos or books within long poems, chapters in books, unpublished theses, and articles:

> 'Ode on a Grecian Urn'
> 'Monody on the Death of Chatterton'
> H. Clough, Amours de Voyage, vii, 'Claude to Eustace'

When a quoted sentence or question is complete and starts with a capital letter, its final punctuation mark should fall within the closing quotation mark. You don't then need to add another punctuation mark outside the quotation:

> 'I am amazed', he wrote, 'at the sauciness of the Bishop of Lincoln.'

> 'What is the use of a book', thought Alice, 'without

pictures or conversations?'

In all other cases – incomplete sentences, phrases, and single words – punctuation follows the final quotation mark:

> Two weeks later he left London 'to escape this intolerable heat'.

> At the bottom of the letter was written the single word 'Bum'.

Note the placing of the comma in the following examples of direct speech:

> 'Give this', he said, 'to your sister.'
> (= Give this to your sister.)

> 'Sit down,' she said, 'and listen to me carefully.'
> (= Sit down, and listen to me carefully.)

> 'No,' he said. 'I prefer to remain where I am.'
> (= No. I prefer to remain where I am.)

DAY 10

That which does not kill you

You think that there is a hard and fast rule of grammar that everyone ought to obey. Then, when you look closely, you discover it isn't a rule at all. It was a handy guide that has been so rigorously protected that it has fossilised.

In some ways, choosing whether to use **which** and when to use **that** is such a curious fossil. Here is the traditional rule:

> Use **that** when the extra information about the subject is essential to the sense of the sentence.

> Use **which** if it's an interesting but non-essential piece of information.

So this is correct:

> Cars that use hybrid technology are good news for the planet.

This is wrong:

> Cars, which use hybrid technology, are good news for the planet.

Because if you took out the 'which use hybrid technology' clause, you would have 'Cars are good news for the planet.' Not really true.

However this is fine:

> Cars, which usually have four wheels, are America's most popular mode of transport.

The four wheels clause isn't essential. So we use **which**.

Technically, the rule says, we should use **that** with defining (or restrictive) clauses and **which** for non-defining (or non-restrictive) clauses.

Here's the bad news: one half of the rule, and one half only, is spot on. Using **that** with a non-defining clause sounds odd:

> He produced no more literary work that was a great disappointment to his many admirers.

It clearly should be:

> He produced no more literary work, which was a great disappointment to his many admirers.

The good news is that most of the time your brain doesn't need to be told when to use **which** like this, you naturally write that way.

But the other half of the rule is simply bogus. It's fine to use **which** to introduce a restrictive relative clause:

> The wellies which cost £2,000 were hideous.

Sometimes which is the only option, such as in the title of this chapter. The rule has been regularly violated for centuries by the greatest of literary authorities:

> 'Render therefore unto Caesar the things which are Caesar's' – the King James Bible

> 'I think, if you did that, it would help the deception which we are practising on these bees.' – A.A. Milne (well, Pooh Bear)

How to decide

Hang on, though. Now there are no rules at all? Well, instead of thinking about **that** and **which**, instead decide whether to pin your clause to the subject or not.

Can your phrase be left out without the general sense changing? Would you pause just before you spoke it? And emphasise it slightly? Then set it off with commas, or dashes or parentheses.

> The flooded Edinburgh pub, which didn't open on Hogmanay, missed out on a serious cash windfall.

With that done, you can stop fretting about **that** and **which** – unless you are John Dryden you are naturally going to use **which**.

But if your phrase is vitally important to the subject of the sentence:

> Every Edinburgh pub **which didn't open on Hogmanay** missed out on a serious cash windfall.

Such as here, where if you leave out the bold phrase, you change the meaning. And if you don't emphasise it in your speech, then don't set it off with punctuation.

Now your **which** and **that** choice is also simple. Fire ahead and go for **which** if it sounds good, but you can never go wrong if you choose **that**.

DAY 11

For example, should I use i.e. or e.g.?

It's easy to get these two abbreviations mixed up, but they are not interchangeable.

Here's how to tell them apart:

e.g. means **for example**. It is an abbreviation of the Latin phrase **exempli gratia** (literally, for example).

> There are many delicious Scottish beers, e.g. Deuchars IPA.

i.e. means **that is to say**. It is an abbreviation of the Latin phrase id est (literally, **that is**).

> Richard is feeling delicate today, i.e. he's hungover.

The way I remember it is that e.g. is nearly egg and that is **an eggsample** of something.

One final thing - you should always include the dots:

> It is e.g. not eg

Until the eighteenth century, Latin was the universal language of European academia. After that the local mother tongues dominated, but many Latin phrases hung on because they are useful. You will still see these abbreviations:

A.D. (anno Domini) – in the year of our Lord
a.m. (Ante Meridiem) – before midday
(circa) – about, around. Often seen with dates: c.
1850
cf. (confer) – bring together, compare
C.V. (curriculum vitae) – course of life. So, a list of
stuff that you are pretending to have done. In the
USA this is a résumé.
et al. (et alii, or et alia, or et alibi) – and others, and
other things, and other places
etc. (et cetera) – and the rest
et seq. (et sequens) – that which follows
ibid. (ibidem) – in the same place. Often seen in
footnotes.
infra dig (infra dignitatum) – beneath one's dignity
N.B. (nota bene) – note well
p.a. (per annum) – through a year
per cent. (per centum) – for each hundred
P.M. (Post Meridem) – after midday
P.S. (post scriptum) – after what has been written
Q.E.D. (quod erat demonstrandum) – which was to
be demonstrated
R.I.P. (requiescat in pace) – may he/she rest in peace
sic. (sic erat scriptum) – thus it was written. Used
when your source made a mistake and you haven't
mistyped.
stat. (statim) – immediately. If the doctor writes that
on your chart with an exclamation mark, call your
loved ones.
v. (vide) – see. Also v. infra – see below, v. supra – see
above.
viz. (videlicet) – namely. Also a rude magazine. N.B.
vis-à-vis is from French and means face-to-face.

vs or v. (versus) – against

Where possible, however, try to use English equivalents (e.g. 'see above' rather than v. supra, 'namely' rather than 'viz.') and avoid beginning a sentence with e.g. or i.e.

DAY 12

A capital crime

We all know that proper names need a capital letter. But is the government a proper thing? Who knows.

The golden rule is: when in doubt about capitalization, use a capital for the particular and a small letter for the general.

When you are talking about specific institutions, organizations, denominations, and political/cultural movements, you need a capital letter:

> Anglican
> the Army/Navy/Air Force
> the Bank of England
> the Bar
> the Cabinet
> the Church of England
> Communism
> the Conservative Party
> the Crown
> Cubism
> the Government (i.e. a specific body of persons)
> Impressionism
> Marxism
> Presbyterian
> Roman Catholic
> Romanticism
> the State

but use lower case for normal adjectival use:

> catholic sympathies
> conservative in outlook
> a democratic organization
> a government spokesperson
> the novel was romantic in conception
> socialist tendencies

Capitalize days of the week, months, festivals, and holidays:

> Monday
> October
> Passover
> Easter
> New Year's Day
> the Fifth of November

but use lower case for seasons:

> spring
> summer
> autumn
> winter

Capitalize geological periods/formations and historical periods/events:

> Carboniferous
> Pleistocene
> Bronze Age
> Stone Age
> Middle Ages (but lower case for medieval)

Renaissance
First World War
the Last Supper

Capitalize titles of rank, office-holders, and nicknames:

King Henry
the Duke of Wellington
the Prince of Wales
the Archbishop of Canterbury
the Master of Christ's
Major-General
Vice-President
the Prime Minister
the Pope
the French Ambassador
the Lake Poets
the Apostles

but use lower case when referring to a title in a general sense:

every king of England
all the dukes and earls
most prime ministers
a French ambassador
seventeenth-century popes

Capitalize compass directions when they denote a titular geographical/political region:

Northern Ireland (but northern England)
the East
the West End

Capitalize words derived from proper nouns where the identity of the noun is clear:

> Shakespearean
> Homeric
> Dickensian
> Christianize

but use lower case where the identity is obscure or has become conventional:

> boycott
> chauvinistic
> pasteurize
> wellington boots

Generally capitalize adjectives based on nationality:

> French polish
> Dutch oven
> Irish setter
> German measles

The Bible should always take an initial capital when referring to the collection of sacred texts itself; use lower case when referring to individual copies:

> The Authorized Version of the Bible was published in 1611.
> He placed a bible on the table.

Also use lower case for the adjective 'biblical'.

DAY 13

Misuses and misspellings

Some words are just tricky to spell. Others sound very similar to each other and you can easily muddle up their meanings.

Here are some of the most common misuses and misspellings to watch out for:

Common misuses

>   adverse (unfavourable, antagonistic)
>   averse (disinclined, opposed to)
>
>   casual (relaxed)
>   causal (having an effect on something)
>
>   complement (fits well with
>   compliment (saying something nice)
>
>   dependant (noun, someone who depends on another)
>   dependent (adjective, relying on something else)
>
>   deprecate (express disapproval)
>   depreciate (to decline in value)
>
>   duel (to fight)
>   dual (twin)
>
>   except (leave out)

accept (to receive as adequate)

loose (of morals)
lose (the game)

loth (unwilling)
loath (detest)

principal (can be an adjective meaning 'main' or a
noun meaning a leader)
principle (always a noun meaning moral rule)

Scotch whisky has no e
Irish whiskey does

Common misspellings

Use **onto** (one word) except where on is an independent
adverb:

They drove onto the beach.
He walked onto the station platform.

but:

They continued on to the beach.
He walked on to the next station.

affect means 'to have an influence on, make a difference to'
(or sometimes 'to pretend')
effect means 'to bring about, cause something to happen'
(verb) or 'consequential change' (noun):

These measures chiefly affect the elderly.
It does not affect me.

The prisoner effected his escape.
The measures had an adverse effect.

Until has one l.
Till has two.

They are interchangeable in most situations. An exception is when setting up a negative conditional:

> Until my landlord fixes the plumbing, I am not going to pay the rent.

Till would not work so well here.

Finally, never write *'til*.

Till is actually the older of the two words, and *until* was derived from it rather than the other way round.

Contronyms

English being slightly eccentric, there are some words that mean one thing – and the complete and utter opposite thing at the same time. Brilliant.

> **To cleave** can mean **to cling** or **to split**.
> **To dust** can mean **to remove dust** (cleaning a house) or **to add dust** (e.g. to dust a cake with powdered sugar).

Inflammable technically means **capable of burning** but is commonly taken to mean **unburnable**.
Oversight means **supervision; an oversight** means **not noticing something**.
Pass on can mean **reject from** and **continue through a process** (e.g. Let's pass on this candidate).
To rent can mean **to borrow from** or **to lend to**.
To replace can mean **to place back where it was** or **substitute with something else**.
To sanction can mean **to permit** or **to punish**.
To screen can mean **to show** or **to conceal**.
To go off can mean **to begin to make a noise** (e.g. The alarm went off) or **stop operating** (e.g. The alarm went off by itself).

Tricky words

Even the best of us get some of these stinkers wrong:

> accommodate (there is plenty of room inside for Cs and Ms)
> acquire
> acquit
> bureaucracy (a pain in the arse in itself, and to spell)
> conscience
> conscious
> diarrhoea (diarrhea in America)
> census but consensus (remember that the census does not require a consensus, because they are not related)
> definitely
> desert

dessert (you want two desserts, so put two Ss in)

dumbbell (even clever people forget one of the Bs)

embarrass

exhilarate

harass

jewellery (in Britain, jewelry in the USA)

judgment (traditionally there has only ever been one E in it)

kernel (of a nut)

colonel (is not nutty, he's very sensible)

idiosyncrasy (not idiosyncracy)

liaise (so note the preposterous number of Is in liaising – three!)

manoeuvre*

millennium (not millennium)

minuscule (sounds like it should be 'mini-scule'. But it isn't)

mischievous

pastime (there should be two Ts, but there aren't. One died ages ago.)

phlegm

privilege (two Is, two Es, too rich for you)

restaurant (I can spell restaurant just like my aunt, while the rest-a-u-rant that you can't!)

rhyme (this was spelled 'rime' until 1650, then people started mucking about with it to make it look like rhythm)

rhythm

sapphire (note the two Ps)

supersede (This word supersedes all others in oddness. It's the only English word with this sound spelled –sede.)

threshold (only two Hs)

weather (it's raining)
whether (or not it's ever going to stop raining)

*Americans have sorted this bastard out by simply changing it to 'maneuver'.

DAY 14

Passive aggressive

The passive voice should never be used.

This sentence is contradicting itself – it is in the passive voice. So what's the problem here?

Well, this is another occasion where breaking the 'rule' is not grammatically wrong. It is a style choice.

Passive voice is when the object of a sentence ends up looking more like the subject. In the above example, because we have set off with the 'passive voice' as our subject we have to contort the verb a bit. We have said 'be used' rather the more active 'use'. The true subject, 'you', has also disappeared.

Passive sentences seem to lie about the place like a stoned flatmate. You want to grab them and shake a bit of life into them.

Luckily, this is easy to do. We just need to find that subject and put it first. The sentence then becomes more engaging:

You should never use the passive voice.

That runs subject-verb-object, which is the clearest way of writing.

Sometimes people write in the passive voice because they think it sounds more formal. But really it just sounds stiff and pompous.

> The new policy was approved by the board members.

Come on, that's woolly. How about:

> The board members approved the new policy.

Simple is your friend.

The passive voice also crops up a lot in business because its little reversing trick seems to take away the responsibility for an action.

> Cigarette advertising was created that appealed to children.

We think: 'Oh, that sounds awful. I wonder which terrible people did that?' The 'was created' has waved a magic wand at that sentence and made its subject disappear. However, when we look at what is really being said:

> We created cigarette advertising that appealed to children.

'You! It was you lot, you bastards!'

Watch out for that sort of nonsense...

When to use the passive voice

The passive voice does have definite uses, for example if the thing being acted on is the main attraction:

> The unknown victim was robbed around midnight.

You don't want to write:

> The robber robbed the unknown victim around
> midnight.

Another example is when the subject is not important or is a non-specific person:

> The northern lights can be seen in the early hours of
> the morning.

is passive. But beware:

> You can see the northern lights in the early hours of
> the morning.

'Can I? But I live in Paris.' The sentence is hypothetical. You don't want it grounded with too much reality, or it will lose its meaning.

You can use passive voice in technical and scientific writing:

> Current was then applied to the apparatus.

is fine. You don't need to write:

> I then applied current to the apparatus.

You sound like a mad professor confessing his crazy experiments.

Passive voice is sometimes hard to spot. But Microsoft Word helpfully puts a green squiggle under it and offers you alternatives. Have a look at these. Often they are much livelier.

Finally, you don't need to worry about this, but not all verbs can be made passive. Only transitive verbs (those that take objects) can do this. Intransitive verbs (such as lie, go and sneeze) can't. You can't turn:

John went to bed.

into

Bed was went to by John.

Unless you're a pothead flatmate, of course.

DAY 15

A singular problem

> We offer a range of products that include beans and peas.

This sentence is wrong. The problem arose because we have a singular noun (a range of products) that mistakenly becomes a plural in the mind of the writer.

The phrase a range of products sounds like a plural bunch of things. But, in the eyes of the English language, it is a singular entity (a range). Therefore, the sentence should read:

> We offer a range of products that includes beans and peas.

Here are some more examples of singular things that are commonly mistaken for plurals:

> The couple were married by Father Jack. X
> The couple was married by Father Jack. ✔
>
> The series of films were directed by Spielberg. X
> The series of films was directed by Spielberg. ✔
>
> Wayne Rooney's team are playing away next week. X
> Wayne Rooney's team is playing away next week. ✔
>
> Scottish Widows have a range of products. X
> Scottish Widows has a range of products. ✔

DAY 16

I say, your modifier appears to be dangling

Consider the sentence:

> As a Halifax customer, we hope you are enjoying your premium banking service.

If you read this closely you will see that the subject of the sentence drifts. It seems to start as a Halifax customer but then becomes we, the people doing the hoping. This is clearly not what the writer intended.

A phrase like this is called a dangling or misplaced modifier and you should generally avoid them. Try simply:

> We at Halifax hope you are enjoying your premium banking service.

Here's another example:

> Flitting gaily from flower to flower, the soldier watched the bee.

That's an interesting mental image. Try simply:

> The soldier watched the bee flitting gaily from flower to flower.

But before the Grammar Trappers start the fist pumps, dangling modifiers aren't always grammatical errors.

Many participles have become prepositions:

> **according**, **allowing**, **concerning**, **considering**,
> **excepting**, **following**, **given**, **granted**, **owing**,
> **regarding** and **respecting**.

They don't need subjects at all. Also, a modifier can dangle when its implied subject is the writer and the reader. Look at these examples:

> Considering that the whole idea behind poetry is to convey meaning through sound, 'Jabberwocky' is actually a brilliant work of art.

> Given that the profit margin is high on derivatives trading, Cookie Monster's estimates seem to be somewhat low.

> Assuming this flaming meeting ever starts, it may still go somewhere.

Jabberwocky is not considering. **Cookie Monster's estimates** are not given. **It** is not assuming.

If you try to stick **we find**, **we see** or another subject into the main clause to avoid a dangler, then the sentence becomes cluttered or its meaning shifts:

> If we agree that the whole idea behind poetry is to convey meaning through sound, 'Jabberwocky' is actually a brilliant work of art.

Whether to rewrite a sentence with a dangler is a matter

of judgment, not grammar. Just consider these points. Is the dangler ambiguous?

> When a small boy, a girl is of little interest.

Does the reader have to search for the meaning, thus slowing their progress down? Is this a formal document that will be closely scrutinised? Alternatively, does using a dangler actually help your sentence do what it needs to?

> Considering where I woke up, my aftershave choice was a good one.

my aftershave choice wasn't doing any considering. The true sense is more:

> If one considers where I woke up, my aftershave choice was a good one.

But imagine if a stand-up comedian spoke these lines. Given the tone and subject, the first version is funnier and more apt. (Did you notice that this last sentence is also a dangler!?)

Sometimes you can dare to dangle...

DAY 17

Fulfil your skill

When full is added to a word to form an adjective, you knock the second **l** off:

> doubtful
> fruitful

Sometimes you also knock off the last letter of the word itself:

> awful (awe-full)
> skilful (skill-full)

Fulfil (full-fill) also follows this rule, as does fulfilment. But when it becomes fulfilling or fulfilled it gets its second l back.

Note: it's the turn of our American cousins to be illogical on this one – they follow our spellings for doubtful, awful and skilful but use fulfill instead of fulfil. Go figure.

DAY 18

It's either wrong or its not, right?

Here's the simple rule:

YOU ONLY USE AN APOSTROPHE WHEN **IT'S** IS A CONTRACTION OF **IT IS**:

> It's a really hot day and I am thirsty. (It's instead of it is.)

Never when it indicates possession:

> I'm dreaming of The Jolly Judge and its excellent range of drinks.

Here **its** refers to the range of drinks belonging to the Monkey Bar. If you replaced it with **it is**, it wouldn't make sense:

> I'm dreaming of The Jolly Judge and it is excellent range of drinks.

That's the quick way of remembering it – put **it is** in place instead of **its** and if there's no sense there's no apostrophe.

The reason for this is that **its** is a possessive pronoun, like **his, theirs, ours** and **hers**. They already indicate possession, so they don't need a possessive apostrophe:

> Steve scratched his head.

Humans are the only animals that have children
on purpose with the exception of guppies, who like
to eat theirs. (P J O'Rourke)

The dog licked its unmentionables.

Note the use of both **its** and **it's** here:

I'm dreaming of The Jolly Judge and its excellent
range of drinks. It's making me want to get the
hell out of this library.

Note: **It's** is also a valid contraction of **it has**, as in:

It's been a long time since I rock and rolled
Been a long time since I did the strrrroll…

Sorry, I'd better stop there.

DAY 19

Toodle-pip

Traditionally, if you begin a letter by addressing someone by **name**, you should sign it off with **Yours sincerely**.

If you begin a letter with a **generic salutation**, you should end it with the valediction **Yours faithfully**. So we have these pairs of examples:

> Dear Ms Reynolds,
> Yours sincerely,

> Dear Julie,
> Yours sincerely,

and

> Dear Sir/Madam,
> Yours faithfully,

> Dear colleague,
> Yours faithfully,

Please note that the words sincerely and faithfully do not normally require capital letters.

> Sincerely yours

is an American variant, but you shouldn't freely swap it with Yours sincerely; it has a more intimate tone.

Yours truly

is a good option if you're writing professional correspondence to a named recipient, but neither Yours faithfully or Yours sincerely are appropriate

Dear Mr. Spielberg
Yours truly,
Siskel & Ebert

However, these days we are far more likely to write an email to someone and the salutations above can seem overly formal in such a medium. Best wishes is the most popular of the acceptable valedictions, and it suits all salutations:

Dear customer,
Best wishes,
The Tesco Customer Service Team

Dear Mr Cruise,
Best wishes,
Floyd Proudhomme
General Manager
The Centurion Sauna

Regards is becoming more popular as a semi-formal valediction in emails. While

Kind regards

and

Best regards

are good for friends or loved ones, or a close working

relationship. But don't use these in formal letters.

Other expressions are appropriate in less formal situations, including versions of **Best wishes** such as

> All my best

or, simply:

> Best

For family members or intimates, an expression such as

> Your friend
> Your loving son

or (in the case of lovers):

> Your Jonny

may be used. Or the name may simply be preceded with **All my love** or **Love**.

Yours fraternally is a common valediction in the Labour movement.

If, like me, you find **Yours sincerely** and **Yours faithfully** to be so standard as to be boring, you can always make go back in time to find some lovely formal ones:

> I beg to remain, Sir, your most humble and obedient servant.

Or if you're writing to pals, why not have some fun and make one up?

> Until your reply rouses me once more, I remain, dozing, yours,
> Mr Dougal Dormouse

> Yours aye

is a Scottish phrase meaning 'yours always'. It has a lovely ring to it and is a great favourite of pirates.

DAY 20

Conjunctionitis

You can't start a sentence with 'and' – so said your old English teacher. Well, you can.

And that's all there is to it.

Okay, there's a bit more to it than that. This rule made sense once upon a time. When you were eight years old your thoughts spilled straight out of your head onto the page:

> On Saturday I went to football with Daddy
> and scored a goal so I got a Happy Meal and Daddy
> had one too but said not to tell Mummy because
> she said he was not to also we went to Granny's
> house and she made stew so Daddy and me had to
> eat two lunches and...

Teachers needed to show you how to break up your thoughts into chunks. But if you just scatter full stops into that paragraph it will read just as badly. By steering kids away from starting every thought with **and, because, but, or, so, also** we train them to structure interesting prose.

But we're not eight now. We've learned how to vary our writing, how to develop an argument logically, and how to build to a climax. Prepositions are invaluable tools in linking individual sentences into interesting passages. You can use them to start a sentence if the clauses being connected are too long or complicated to run on into a very long sentence.

Consider the Star Wars music. You're watching the slow opening credits crawl, then suddenly, from nowhere:

PFWARP!!

A truncated blast more suited to a tune's climax. All wrong, surely? No, it does a great job. It grabs your attention and alerts you to something very new.

Just like John Williams' music, conjunctions can be used to good effect at the start of sentences. When you put a conjunction at the start of a sentence you create a different feeling:

> Luke was prepared to help his uncle for another season. But he hadn't reckoned on the Empire.

Here we have a have a short introductory sentence, then a definite pause. Then a punchy, second sentence that leaps up and reverses what went before. It's dramatic. But it also starts a sentence with but. So let's avoid that and see what happens:

> Luke was prepared to help his uncle for another season, but he hadn't reckoned on the Empire.

The pause here is smaller and the surprise is weaker. If you miss the pause, what else could you do to avoid breaking this 'rule'? You could try another linking word:

> Luke was prepared to help his uncle for another season. However, he hadn't reckoned on the Empire.

Gah! **However** is weaker. It tells you that something

surprising is on the way, but at the same time it lessens that surprise. It's not punchy. It sounds stuffy and like something from a legal document. **But** just hits you. **But** is better.

But, but, but... sentence fragments!!!

The Grammar Trappers get a little worked up about starting sentences with a conjunction because they fear it will turn that sentence into a fragment. Firstly, every great writer since about 1850 has used sentence fragments. You don't want to write them in a legal document, but in fiction they are indispensible for varying pace and mood.

However, let's pretend for a moment that we do want to avoid them absolutely. The first thing to know is that there are three different **types** of conjunctions:

Coordinating, which you can remember with the mnemonic FANBOYS:

> For, And, Nor, But, Or, Yet, So.

Correlative, which come in pairs. For example:

> neither/nor, either/or, both/and, not only/but also, rather/or

and **Subordinating**. And it's only this last kind that can turn a clause into a fragment. Subordinating conjunctions include:

> **if**, **because**, **although**, **when**, and many others.

Coordinating conjunctions can combine two clauses to make a sentence. And they can prefix a single clause to make that a sentence.

Subordinating conjunctions are different. The theory is that if you pop one of these bad boys on the start of a single clause you get a sentence fragment:

> Because I was stressed.

is a fragment: **because** sits on the front of only one clause

> I was stressed.

But:

> I went to play golf because I was stressed.

is a complete sentence, with **because** joining two clauses: **I went to play golf** and **I was stressed**.

However, even this isn't always a problem!

Because starts some of the most-frequently used sentences in modern English, answers to **why** questions:

> Why can't I have an X-box?
> Because I said so.

It can be a deliberate stylistic choice, giving a teasing explanation to a main clause that is still in the post. You could say:

I walk the line, because you're mine.

but

Because you're mine, I walk the line.

Is far more poetic and memorable.

The Golden Rule here is: Don't Worry About Conjunctions At The Start Of Sentences. It's simply not worth the trouble.

Finally, just to be extra clear about this, I'm going to call in the big guns and quote directly from the Chicago Manual of Style:

> 'There is a widespread belief—one with no historical or grammatical foundation—that it is an error to begin a sentence with a conjunction such as and, but or so. In fact, a substantial percentage (often as many as 10 percent) of the sentences in first-rate writing begin with conjunctions. It has been so for centuries, and even the most conservative grammarians have followed this practice.

DAY 21

Prepositions and where you can stick them

> We are such stuff as dreams are made on.

is one of Shakespeare's most quoted (and most misquoted, but that's another matter) lines. Utter it and English teachers and literature aficionados will half close their eyes and drift off into a reverie about its power and poetry.

Until you point out to them that it is ungrammatical. For it ends on a preposition and that, as the grammar Nazis shriek, is something that you must never, ever do. Right?

In case you're not sure what preposition is, I have a handy aide-memoire. This is going to sound crude, but I swear you'll remember it forever. A preposition is, generally, anywhere you can place a dildo:

> up, down, behind, around, by, through, after, in, to, on, with, etc.

So, who do you think is right, the greatest writer who has ever held a pen or shrieking grammar Nazis? Duh, it's Shakespeare.

Because this rule isn't a rule at all, it's a wet fart brewed up by an envious John Dryden in 1672 and blown at Ben Jonson in an effort to show that Jonson stank as a poet. Dryden used a half-baked analogy with Latin to show that prepositions shouldn't lie at the end of clauses. But Latin's equivalent to a preposition is bolted to the noun and can't be put anywhere else even if you had a chisel.

There is nothing, ABSOLUTELY NOTHING, grammatically incorrect with ending a sentence with a preposition.

This is a style issue. If the sentence sounds better with the preposition elsewhere, then move it. If not, let it be, for pity's sake.

The better to see you with.

It's you she's thinking of.

are fine the way they are. And Travis Bickle may have been a murderous weirdo but he wasn't ungrammatical. As he talked to himself in his mirror he said:

I'm the only one here. Who the fuck do you think you're talking to?

You might be tempted to rearrange this to:

I'm the only one here. To whom the fuck do you think you're talking?

which obeys Dryden's preposition 'rule', but is so wrong wrong wrong for this piece of writing.

Occasionally when you a preposition can seem stranded at the end of a sentence, if the word is too lightweight to be the sentence's focal point.

> Where are you at?

Sounds weak. It's much better just to say:

> Where are you?

Of course, flip that thought around and if you need the preposition to deliver the crucial punch of meaning of the sentence then you should actively place it at the end.

> Something to guard against.
> It's nothing to sneeze at.
> Happer doesn't know what he's talking about.

One good thing has come from this mythical preposition rule. If you start trying to move prepositions from the ends of sentences where they're perfectly happy, you magically learn how to talk like Yoda:

> The vodka had not even been paid for.
> Paid for the vodka had not even been.

> All the guys had to run away.
> Away all the guys had to run.

> The stag do had to be called off.
> Called off the stag do had to be.

Finally, if some smarty-pants continues to insist that you cannot put a preposition at the end of a sentence, ask them to correct this one:

Look what the cat dragged in.

DAY 22

Whom the hell do you think you are?

The writer Calvin Trillin said,

> As far as I'm concerned, "whom" is a word that was invented to make everyone sound like a butler.

He has a point. If you use it too much, you can sound pompous and stuffy rather than erudite. That's because in many ways it is archaic.

Linguists have counted the frequency of **whom** in 200 years of printed texts (well, their computers have) and have found that its use has measurably declined.

But its *rate* of decline has held steady since the 1980s. So **whom** still has its uses, and looks like it always will. For example, there are many occasions where it adds clarity:

> Who's dating whom?

It occurs in standard expressions that we still use happily:

> To whom it may concern…
> With whom do you wish to speak?

What about in normal speech? It's a good idea to learn how it should be used. The very basic rule is that **who** refers to the subject of a sentence and **whom** to the object. This works in the same way as **he** and **him**, **she** and **her**.

So if someone said to you:

> **Who** drank my last beer?

You would obviously say:

> **He** did.

not

> Him did.

And if they said:

> **Whom** should I get to go to the off licence?

You'd say:

> Get **him** to go.

not

> Get he to go.

In the first example the person drinking the beer was the subject. So we were referred to them using **he** and **who**. In the second example the person being forced to go to the off licence (presumably the same selfish bugger) was the object, so we referred to them with **him** and **whom**.

The choice between using

> who and whom

is exactly the same as that between using

> he and him

or

> she and her

Try remembering:

> Who/he
> Whom/him

However, whether the strict grammarians like it or not, once something starts to sound pompous to lots of people, that connotation is very difficult to shake. Here's an example. We say:

> **Damian** shagged my girlfriend.

So we ask:

> **Who** shagged my girlfriend?

We say:

> Damian shagged **her**.

So we ask:

> **Whom** did Damian shag?

and we are using **whom** accurately, but it's so out of place with the tone and subject of the writing that it sounds laughably pompous. This is one of the places where **whom** has died for a reason.

You may see **whom** being used when people want to sound respectable and knowledgeable. Instead, they get it wrong:

> Whomever created this business plan did not accurate take into account the prodigious initial investment required.

Some people drop whom into their speech to sound posh. They may be correct, but is it worth it? For example, you may think you are being impressively correct if you say to someone:

> Whom are you going to believe, me or your own eyes?

But your listener will think you're a 12-bore idiot. Likewise:

> It's not what you know; it's whom you know.
> Do you know whom you're talking to?

Generally, then, avoid **whom** in short questions and relative clauses to avoid doing a butler impression.

But don't be afraid to use it at any other time, even in informal speech and writing, if it adds clarity or meaning to your sentences.

DAY 23

There ... Their ... They're

This is easily one of the most common mistakes in English. So don't sweat it!

Most of the time most people pronounce these words the same. They are homophones. Interestingly, they aren't as EXACTLY identical in sound as **deer** and **dear** are, for example. Say this slowly and clearly:

> They're going to their house over there.

The final 'there' will have much more of an 'eh' sound, particularly if you're Scottish.

However, the point is that it's usually tricky to tell them apart by sound. But they are very different in meaning.

There	Naming a place
Their	Showing ownership
They're	Combining the words they and are

So, to tell them apart every time you have to write one, just pause and ask yourself this question:

What can I replace this problem word with? If you could swap in **another location: to the pub** – then use **there**.

> I have never been… to the pub … before.

I have never been... there ... before.

Sometimes you might need to try swapping in 'where' or 'here' –

... Where... was a problem
... There ... was a problem

Or, f you could swap in **our** – then use **their**.

This is ... our ... roast ox.
This is ... their ... roast ox.

If you could swap in **they are** – then use **they're**.

... They are ... going to have indigestion.
... They're ... going to have indigestion.

While we're on this topic, let's sort out your ... you're.

Your   Showing ownership
You're   Combining the words you and are

So, what can I replace this problem word with? If you could swap in **she's** – then use **you're**.

... She's ... going to go bananas.
... You're ... going to go bananas.

If you could swap in **her** – then use **your**.

Some joker has nicked ... her ... parking space.

Some joker has nicked … your … parking space.

And, finally, let's clear up were… we're… where

Were	Having the quality of being
We're	Combining the words we and are
Where	Naming a place

What can I replace this problem word with? If you could swap in **are** – then use **were**.

My grandparents … are … a disgrace to the family.
My grandparents … were … a disgrace to the family.

If you could swap in **we are** – then use **we're**.

… We are … never going to love down the shame of their behaviour.
… We're … never going to love down the shame of their behaviour.

If you could swap in **another location: in which batch of scrumpy** – then use **where**.

No one even knows … in which batch of scrumpy … they put the cat.

No one even knows … where … they put the cat.

Okay lots of examples there. But the basic idea is to try swapping another word in. The type of word that fits will give you a clue which version of your problem word to use.

DAY 24

Between you and I, this is wrong

You, I, and Me are pronouns that often cause problems. But what exactly are pronouns?

When a movie director is tinkering with his lights he uses stand-ins. These are people who are roughly the same size and shape as Tom Cruise and Emily Blunt, but who cost a lot less money to have standing around all day.

Pronouns are like movie stand-ins.

Imagine, for whatever reason, that you don't want to say Tom Cruise, Emily Blunt or Mr Spielberg. Instead you can use words such as **you**, **I** and **me** (as well as **he**, **we**, **they**, **him**, **her** and **she**, etc.). Instead of saying:

> Tom Cruise is a talented actor. Tom Cruise follows a woo-woo religion.

We say:

> Tom Cruise is a talented actor. He follows a woo-woo religion.

Tom Cruise is a noun. **He** takes the place of this noun. It is a pronoun.

Tom Cruise is also our subject. He is the one doing the acting in the sentence as well as in real life – he is **following** a woo-woo religion.

This means that he is a **subject pronoun**. Literally, a pronoun that takes the place of the subject. Now if we say:

> Tom stars with Emily Blunt.

Emily Blunt is the object. She is being acted on. If we wanted to use a pronoun we could say:

> Tom stars with Emily Blunt. He fights with her.

Her is an **object pronoun**.

Subject and object pronouns will help us understand 'between you and me'. Let's have another example. Do you say:

> Me fancy Emily Blunt.

or

> I fancy Emily Blunt.

It's obviously the second one (unless you are Cookie Monster). **I** am doing the loving so **I** am the subject of the sentence. 'I' is a subject pronoun. But do we say:

> Emily fancies I.

or

> Emily fancies me?

Again, the second one is correct (because I am so hunky). I am the not one 'doing' anything in this sentence. It's Emily who is doing the loving. She is the subject. The object is 'me'. So:

Me is an object pronoun
I is a subject pronoun

The tricky bit comes when 'you' comes along. That's because it works as **both a subject and an object pronoun**:

You love Tom.
Tom loves you.

Both are correct.

More than one pronoun

You may have heard One Direction singing 'You and I don't want to be like them'.

This is **correct**, because you and I are dual subjects. You could take out either pronoun and the sentence would make sense:

You don't want to be like them.
I don't want to be like them.

Between You and Me

Now that we know about subject and object pronouns, we can tackle the phrase between you and I, and see why it's wrong.

Between is a preposition. It describes places or relationships in time and space. Other prepositions include **by, up, above, beside, after,** etc.

The rule is that after a preposition such as between, we use the object pronoun rather than the subject pronoun.

So when the boys in One Direction later sing in that same song:

> Nothing can come between you and I.

they are now being ungrammatical. But they're so perfect! They should have said:

> Nothing can come between you and me.

However, it's easy to see why this mistake crops up so much. People are used to being told that:

> Billy and me got thrown out of the pub

is wrong and should be:

> Bill and I got thrown out of the pub.

(Remember from above that Bill and I are dual subjects. And rowdy ones at that.) They then incorrectly correct:

> between you and me

to

> between you and I.

DAY 25

If I were a waswolf

Verbs have moods. These show a speaker's attitude toward his or her use of that verb. The main moods in English are:

Indicative – showing a state of reality. This is the most common mood:

> The lads are in the pub.

Imperative – showing a state of command:

> Get me a bloody beer.

Interrogative – a state of questioning:

> Why is he taking so bloody long?

Subjunctive – shows doubts, wishes and possibilities:

> If he weren't my brother, I wouldn't bother going out with him.

You use all of these correctly all the time without knowing it, and we don't need to go into too much depth in this guide about moods. But the question of whether to use:

> If I was

or

> If I were

is one that people often ask, and it concerns the subjunctive mood. Here's the golden rule:

> When your sentence uses the subjunctive mood you should use **were** not **was**.

You can spot the subjunctive mood if you see the words **if**, **though**, **that** and **unless** introducing a clause that isn't a full sentence (a subordinate clause).

Let's run through some examples and see how they break down:

> He was a vampire.

This is correct because the verb is used in the indicative mood. The verb 'was' is making a simple statement about the past.

> If I was able, I'd stab him with a stake.

This is incorrect because here 'was' is a supposition, a possibility. The speaker might not be able to do the stabbing. It needs the subjunctive mood. See how the word **if** starts a clause that isn't a whole sentence – **If I was able** – a subordinate clause.

> If he was a vampire, I'd hide garlic in his coffin for a laugh.

Incorrect and unwise. It's expressing another possibility and must take the subjunctive mood.

If he were a vampire, I'd probably not mess with his coffin.

Correct and you're learning.

If I were able, I'd chuck holy water on him.

Correct and good luck to you.

Here's another quick example. Midge Ure was being tuneful but ungrammatical when he sang:

If I **was** a soldier

Had he been singing about his past life in the Royal Engineers he could have said:

When I **was** a soldier.

But this is the subjunctive; it's a **possibility** he's talking about. The line should have been:

If I **were** a soldier.

Some people think that the was/were distinction is circling the drain. But it's important to know that many people don't, and it is still correct to use it.

DAY 26

I'm well confused about good

That's all well and good – except it's not.

People often get confused about when to use well and when to use good. In fact, they are two of the most misused words in the English language, and for new writers they cause significant bother.

It's even more complicated than many accomplished writers think. To make everything clear we need to explore **action verbs** and **linking verbs**.

Action verbs include **run, jump** and **swim**. To describe how an action verb is going you need an adverb. Not an adjective.

Well can be an adverb. Great, let's use it. So you can say:

> Your dog runs **well**.

It is wrong to use good here, because it is an adjective:

> Your dog runs **good**.

No. But we **can** write:

> Your dog is good at crapping on my lawn.

Woah, hang on, you say – **crapping** is an action verb if ever there was one. You're right. But the verb we're interested in here isn't **crapping**, it's **is**, a form of **to be**. And to be is a **linking verb**.

Linking verbs are less about doing anything and more about joining other words together. Linking verbs include **appear**, **seem**, **look**, **become** and verbs that describe senses, such as **smell** and **feel**.

To be is the ultimate linking verb. In this example:

> Your dog is a pest.

is links dog and pest.

After linking verbs we normally use **adjectives** – not adverbs – to deliver more information. **Good** is an adjective.

Unlike with action verbs, you **can** use adjectives such as **good** and **bad** after linking verbs. They are technically called predicate adjectives and they refer to the noun before the linking verb.

So we can say:

> Your dog is good.

But not:

> Your dog craps good.

Nor even:

> Your dog craps real good.

But this is fine:

> Your dog **is** good at crapping.

because that linking verb **is** has popped in there before the **good**.

This is why, although **good** is primarily an adjective, we can say:

> I am good.
> I feel good.
> I smell good.
> I look good.

Remember, all these are **linking verbs**, and you can use adjectives after linking verbs.

But, to reiterate, we cannot say:

> I run good.
> I jump good.
> I crap good.

because they are **action verbs**.

Another bit of tricksiness is that **well** strolls about the place with two hats on. It can be both an **adverb** and a **predicate adjective**. So it can be used with both action and linking verbs. In this sentence:

> He runs well.

well is an adverb that describes how he runs. It follows an action verb. But when you say:

> I am well.

well is a predicate adjective. It comes after a linking verb and so is okay here as well.

One last complication

A few verbs (including the sensing verbs) can act as both linking verbs and action verbs. Here's how to spot that.

> Can you replace the verb in question with a form of **to be**?

If you can, it's usually a linking verb. For example, let's check:

> The dog smelled bad.

Can we say:

> The dog was bad. (yes)

So **smelled** here is a linking verb.

Now let's try:

> The dog smelled the man's boots.

Can we say:

> The dog was the man's boots. (no)

No. So **smelled** here was an action verb.

The difference is important. You might think we have to write:

> The dog feels badly about all the crapping it did.

But we don't:

> The dog feels bad about all the crapping it did.

Is perfectly correct because here feels is a linking verb describing how something is. Bad is an adjective.

If we said:

> The dog feels badly because its paw-pads aren't very sensitive.

You get the sense the dog is groping around. This is an action form of the verb feel and so we need to use **badly**, an adjective.

DAY 27

Like, as if

Winston tastes good, like a cigarette should.

So ran a cigarette ad in 1954. It sounds pretty unremarkable. But this ad caused the equivalent of a Twitter storm of its day.

Not for its use of a catchy slogan to take up smoking, but because it was apparently grammatically incorrect. Intellectuals, writers and newspaper editors gave the ad a roasting.

Their beef was that **like** should never be used before a clause. It is not a conjunction. It is a preposition, and it needs a noun. You need to be comparing one thing to another thing:

Do you think my cat looks like me?

The slogan, according to these geniuses, should have been:

Winston tastes good, as a cigarette should.

They were talking like they had air for brains.

Writers have been using **like** with a clause for 600 years. Good ones too, including William Shakespeare, Charles Dickens, Mark Twain, HG Wells and William Faulkner.

But this remains a very deeply held myth. The Grammar Trappers will insist you cannot say:

> It looks like it will rain.

It should be:

> It looks as if it will rain.

But hang on. Even Pooh Bear knows that when you are trying to fool bees you have to say:

> 'Tut-tut, it looks like rain!'

Not:

> 'Tut-tut, it looks as if it will rain!'

That would never fool the bees.

You might be starting to sense that this is another 'error' that isn't an error at all, but a style choice. And you'd be right. **As** is simply more formal. You are free to choose it or the more informal **like** whenever you like.

A similar myth is that you cannot use **like** to introduce examples, like:

> Many advertising copywriters have gone on to be first-class fiction authors, like Salman Rushdie, F. Scott Fitzgerald and Dorothy Sayers.

They insist it should be:

Many advertising copywriters have gone on to be first-class fiction authors, such as Salman Rushdie, F. Scott Fitzgerald and Dorothy Sayers.

Again, though, it comes down to a choice of tone. **Such as** sounds more formal than **like**. You can write either.

DAY 28

She's only a little bit pregnant, Dad

My child is very unique.

What you mean she can juggle five flaming clubs while reciting pi to 3,000 places? Or, she can sing 'Let It Go' vaguely in tune while doing a little dance? Or her DNA does not match the DNA of any other creature that has ever existed or ever will?

The Grammar Trappers get very irate about **very unique**. Their point is that **unique** means:

> Being the only one of its kind; unequaled,
> unparalleled or unmatched.

And that is an absolute state. Like being married, or pregnant. You cannot be a little bit pregnant. Nor **quite, very, almost, rather** or **somewhat** pregnant.

It is binary. Like a light switch. On or off.

There are other things that they claim you cannot modify:

> complete, eternal, absolute, equal and perfect

You cannot be **more certain** about something. You are either certain or you are not. But the American Constitution, a very carefully worded document, aims for:

a more perfect union.

And, when you look at this 'rule' it turns out that lots of excellent writers have been varying absolutes for centuries, often for very deliberate effect.

nothing could be more certain

Is that a modified absolute? Yes, but you have to look carefully.

The problem with the logic is that you **can** have different levels of uniqueness.

Let's say look at your daughter. Unless she is an identical twin, her DNA is unique. No one else's matches it. But 7 billion people on this planet (minus the identical twins) also have DNA that doesn't match anyone else's. So, paradoxically, having unique DNA is common.

Another example. Let's measure your 6-year-old daughter's height and that of her four best friends. One of her friends is 5 feet tall. She is so tall she is unique in her school year.

But remember, your daughter can juggle five flaming clubs while reciting pi to 3,000 places. No one else in the world can do that.

She is more unique than her friend. Or unique to a more exactly measured degree.

Two peas in a pod look identical to you. Look through a magnifying glass and it is clear that each is unique.

I would also argue that even pregnancy is not an absolute state. If you write:

> She is very pregnant.

I know perfectly well what you mean. She looks like she ate a bowling ball for breakfast.

'Pregnant' carries an awful lot of meaning, imagery and connotations. And these can exist on different scales. Some are absolute, some are not.

One aspect of pregnancy is absolute: you either do or do not have a viable foetus inside you. On or off.

However, another aspect of pregnancy, that of how far along the pregnancy path you are, exists on a scale that runs from 0-9 months. You can measure it.

So **very pregnant** makes total sense, if you think of a woman who is 8.5 months through her term.

> 'I am in the rather unique position of being the son, the grandson, and the great grandson of preachers.'
> Martin Luther King

I'd say he was rather unique, wouldn't you?

DAY 29

For a fewer dollars less

Ah, **less** and **fewer**. This always generates lots of clicks on the Daily Telegraph website when it crops up. So what is the rule?

Can you count it?

> Yes – use few and fewer.
> No – use less.

That's the simplest way of looking at it. So:

> The firm has fewer than ten employees.

But:

> The firm is less successful now that we have only ten employees.

The Grammar Trappers have railed against supermarkets, pointing out that their signs over the express lanes, **Ten Items or Less**, is a heinous grammatical error. We are talking about a countable number of fillet steaks, Waitrose!

The terrified supermarkets have responded and replaced it with a sign saying **Ten Items or Fewer**.

But if you think about it this means you should drive at **fewer than 30 mph** in town. Miles per hour is a countable number of things.

We obviously don't say that, so what is going on here?

The English language is good at helping us visualise amounts of things. We can think about lots of little things, such as **granules** or a continuous amount of stuff, such as **sugar**.

> **Granules** is a plural count noun
> **Sugar** is a mass noun

So far so straightforward. The tricky part comes when you use other words to explain how much of a thing you have. You can use some quantifiers with plural count nouns, but not others. And some sit well beside mass nouns, but not others. A few sit well with both.

> many granules ✓
> much granules ✗
>
> much sugar ✓
> many sugar ✗
>
> more granules ✓
> more sugar ✓

Look, **more** works with count nouns and mass nouns. So surely its opposite, **less**, will too?

> less sugar ✓
> less granules ✗

No, your ear tells you it should be **fewer granules**.

So does that mean the **10 items or fewer** correction is right after all? Let's investigate…

We're counting items, so we want to use a count noun, not a mass noun.

But what if we were counting bicycles?

> Following the robbery, I have one less bicycle.

You would not say:

> Following the robbery, I have one fewer bicycle.

So **less** is okay with a singular count noun. Hmm, that seems to have broken the rule.

Would you say:

> Don't serve her she's less than 21 years old.

or

> Don't serve her she's fewer than 21 years old.

The first one. So less is okay when we're talking about a continual scale of measurement.

Now, let's compare:

> I'm making four thousand pounds less than last year.

with

> I'm making four thousand pounds fewer than last year.

Pounds is definitely countable here. It has a number in front and a plural **s** on the end.

But no one is seriously going to suggest that the second line should be the one you use.

That's because we're not thinking of the pounds as individual things, but as part of a mass – my salary.

Finally, let's get back to the supermarket. The same thing is true here. Yes, you can count the items. But they are part of a mass. Your shopping.

Say the distinction was 10 **kilograms** of items. Should the sign say:

>   10 kg of items or fewer
> or
>   10 kg of items or less

Less, of course. But why? Kilograms are countable! Yes, but when you thinking of weight you don't think of discrete kilograms you think of a total measured weight. Something countable becomes a mass.

Imagine there's a Grammar Trapper behind you in the queue. She counts your items and points out that you have 12, not 10. First – argh! Next, you decide to put two items back. Here's my question:

> Do you have **less** in your basket than you did before? Or **fewer**?

You may have fewer items. But you have less shopping.

There is very definitely a sense that when you present yourself at a checkout, you are doing so bearing a mass of something. Your shopping. And shopping is a mass noun.

Which you can have more or less of. You can't buy **a shopping**; you buy **some shopping**.

It turns out that the whole rule that **fewer** is countable and **less** is uncountable has been traced back to the Merriam-Webster Dictionary of English Usage of 1770. And it wasn't included because it was then a rule but because a single author, Robert Baker, preferred it.

Contrastingly, the Oxford English Dictionary lists a countable **less** in 1481, derived from an Old English usage attested by no less a personage than King Alfred.

So, **less** used to be fine with countables. Then one guy came along and didn't like it much, and his opinion got fossilized into a rule. You see how often that has happened?

Less is actually **recommended** in front of counting nouns that denote distance, amount, or time. You would never, ever say:

> We go on holiday in fewer than four weeks.

or

> Bolt can run the 100 m in fewer than ten seconds.

or

> Describe yourself in 30 words or fewer.

So 10 items or less, in a very real sense, is not wrong.

Is that more or less clear?

DAY 30

Licensed to have a licence

Americans don't need to worry about the **license/licence** difference as they end all these types of words -**ice**. Although knowing this will help them understand why any Brits they know are spelling a whole bunch of words incorrectly.

In British English **license** is the verb:

> He went to the post office to **license** his car.
> Bill was, yet again, ejected from **licensed** premises

And **licence** is the noun:

> Bill lost his driver's **licence** yesterday.
> GCHQ assume they have a **licence** to intercept our email.

Similarly, **practise** in British English is the verb:

> Bill claimed he was a practising Jedi knight.

And **practice** is the noun:

> The wookiee opened a dental practice in Bathgate.

The simple way to remember these is:

> **Ice** is a thing; so if a word has **–ice** on the end it is the noun.

That leaves **-ise** words to be the verbs

Advise/advice are the same:

> Bill was **advised** to seek help. (verb)
> The wookiee sought career **advice**. (noun)

And devise/device:

> Bill **devised** a new plan. (verb)
> The wookiee's tooth drilling **device** was terrifying. (noun)

Here's another odd trans-Atlantic spelling difference:

Brits always take **offence** at the Ministry of **Defence**. Americans take **offense*** at **defense** spending.

(*Although this was recorded as a spelling in Britain as early as 1395.)

While we're here, let's look at **-ise** and **-ize**.

Once upon a time most British editors preferred **-ise** endings and American editors demanded **-ize** endings.

Americans still prefer **-ize**, but both are now correct in British English. Although you should stick to one form throughout your writing. In this book I have chosen the **-ize** form, which is the one used by The Times.

Whichever one you stick with, you should also use it to create

-isation or **-ization** forms.

You should also remember that there are some words that always take **-ise**. That's because their **-ise** wasn't a suffix in its own right, but part of a longer element. They are:

> advertise, advise, analyse, apprise
> chastise, circumcise, comprise, compromise
> demise, despise, devise, disguise
> enfranchise, enterprise, excise, exercise
> franchise
> improvise, incise
> merchandise
> prise (open)
> promise
> revise
> supervise, surmise, surprise
> televise

A handful of verbs also always end in **-yse** in British English.

> analyse
> breathalyse
> catalyse
> dialyse
> electrolyse
> hydrolyse
> paralyse
> psychoanalyse

Americans end these with **-yze**.

If Microsoft Word keeps red-underlining your words, check to see that the your country settings are correct.

DAY 31

Apostrophe catastrophe

I'd obliterate every last one of them. Yes, apostrophes. Considering how much confusion and stress they cause, and how little work they actually do, abolishing them would be a logical step.

However, not everyone is this radical. Some people love apostrophes because they make The Best Grammar Traps In The World! The rules can seem so tricky that people are bound to trip up, fall in and then I can laugh at them MWAH HAH HAH!

> pizza's
> ladie's footwear
> childrens books
> artists materials

All wrong, wrong, wrong, you imbeciles, HAAAAAA!

Now, if these smug fiends are merely complaining to a pub landlord because his chalkboard is advertising:

> wine's by the glass

you can simply throw peanuts at them. However, such a Grammar Trapper may also be reading your CV one day, and the fact is that you want them to take you seriously. That means that you have to use apostrophes correctly.

Luckily, there aren't actually that many rules to remember. There are three, in fact. So you can easily remember them and get on with more interesting things. Like wines by the glass.

Apostrophe Golden Rule 1 – Contractions

Is a letter missing in a shortened word? Then you need an apostrophe.

> **It's happy hour** – is short for **It is happy hour**.

So we need one. Likewise:

> **he'd** for **he would** or **he had**
> **can't** for **can not**
> **They've** for **they have**

If you want to write in a very formal style, it is fitting to use fewer contractions. They are not wrong, but using a lot of them can sound informal. You should never use double contractions such as:

> **she'd've** – for **she would have**

in such writing. But watch out for correct uses such as:

> fo'c'sle (a shortening of forecastle
> ne'er-do-well
> will-o'-the-wisp

Although these days:

> Halloween

is so common it is the standard spelling, you might still see:

> Hallowe'en

a throwback to the fact that this is a contraction of:

> All Hallows' Evening

The following colloquial abbreviations, now part of the language, do not now require an apostrophe, except where they are given in quoted matter:

> bus (not 'bus)
> phone (not 'phone)
> cello (not 'cello)
> flu (not 'flu)

You would not write:

> I went to catch the omnibus.

So if you write:

> I went to catch the 'bus.

you will not sound ultra correct, you will sound like a dickhead.

Apostrophe Golden Rule 2 – Plurals

The simple rule is DON'T.

If you're making something plural you just need the **s**. So we have:

> videos
> pizzas
> wines by the glass

This is also true of proper names:

> There are three Richards in my hockey team.
> Keeping up with the Joneses

And if you are making acronyms, dates or phrases plural:

> He does cheap MOTs.
> the three Rs
> dos and don'ts
> ins and outs
> whys and wherefores
> There was a lot of great rock music in the 1970s.

(Although, if you're writing to Americans, note that they DO use apostrophes in dates: 1970's.)

Sometimes people will say that you need apostrophes to make sense of plural lower case letters, such as:

> Mind your p's and q's

However, a neater way of writing this is simply to use upper case for the letter you are making plural:

> Mind your Ps and Qs

Apostrophe Rule 3 – Possessives

Do you want to show that something belongs to a person, or to another thing? Then you put **'s** on the end:

> Jennifer's lovely smile
> The book's cover

Keep following this when the person doing the owning is plural.

Who owns the shoes? The children. So we have:

> The children's shoes.

This works when the person or thing ends in **s**:

> James's grin
> The bus's wheels

or even two Ss:

> Puss's boots

The tricky ones

When the person or thing ends in s and is a plural we have an apostrophe dangling on its own at the end.

Who owns the studios? A whole group of artists. So:

> the artists' studios

And:

> the Beatles' back catalogue
> the ladies' room
> our neighbours' children
> three weeks' time

This also happens when singular nouns end in an *s* or a *z* sound and combined with **sake:**

> for goodness' sake
> for appearance' sake
> for conscience' sake
> old times' sake (follows this rule but is plural)

When singular people own things, ask yourself if you sound an extra s or z on the end. If not, leave that apostrophe hanging:

> Ulysses' adventures
> Socrates' writings
> Jesus' teachings (though **Jesus's** is acceptable in non-liturgical use)

But if we do say an extra s when we speak a non-classical names ending in an *s* or *z* sound, then we use **'s:**

> Berlioz's
> Dylan Thomas's
> Dickens's
> Keats's

Many business, institutions, and journals have abandoned the apostrophe in their titles:

> Barclays Bank
> Citizens Advice Bureau
> Diners Club
> Harrods

There are no apostrophes in wars known by their duration:

> Seven Years War
> Thirty Years War
> Hundred Years War

There are some cases where you just have to know the individual usage:

> All Souls College
> Bury St Edmunds
> Earls Court
> Johns Hopkins University
> Land's End
> Lord's (Cricket Ground)
> Queens' College, Cambridge (founded by two queens)

> The Queen's College, Oxford (founded by one queen)
> St Albans
> St Andrews
> St James's Palace

The last group of exceptions are pronouns such as **its, ours** and **whose**, which we covered on Day 18.

But quickly, when its is possessive it never uses an apostrophe:

> The cat licked its bottom.

We use it only to show a contraction:

> It's making me feel ill.

PS

Post scriptum dictums

Finally, for a bit of fun, here is a collection of rules that break themselves.

They're actually quite a catchy way of remembering the important things in this course.

> Avoid run-on sentences they are hard to read.
> Don't use no double negatives.
> Use the semicolon properly, always use it where it is appropriate; and never where it isn't.
> Reserve the apostrophe for it's proper use and omit it when its not needed.
> Do not put statements in the negative form.
> Verbs has to agree with their subjects.
> No sentence fragments.
> Proofread carefully to see if you any words out.
> Avoid commas, that are not necessary.
> If you reread your work, you will find on rereading that a great deal of repetition can be avoided by rereading and editing.
> A writer must not shift your point of view.
> Eschew dialect, irregardless.
> And don't start a sentence with a conjunction.
> Don't overuse exclamation marks!!!
> Place pronouns as close as possible, especially in long sentences, as of 10 or more words, to their antecedents.
> Writers should always hyphenate between syllables

and avoid un-necessary hyph-ens.
Write all adverbial forms correct.
Don't use contractions in formal writing.
Writing carefully, dangling participles must be
avoided.
It is incumbent on us to avoid archaisms.
If any word is improper at the end of a sentence, a
linking verb is.
Steer clear of incorrect forms of verbs that have
snuck in the language.
Take the bull by the hand and avoid mixed
metaphors.
Avoid trendy locutions that sound flaky.
Never, ever use repetitive redundancies.
Everyone should be careful to use a singular
pronoun with singular nouns in their writing.
If I've told you once, I've told you a thousand times,
resist hyperbole.
Also, avoid awkward or affected alliteration.
Don't string too many prepositional phrases
together unless you are walking through the valley
of the shadow of death.
Always pick on the correct idiom.
"Avoid overuse of 'quotation "marks."'"
The adverb always follows the verb.
Last but not least, avoid cliches like the plague; seek
viable alternatives.

ALSO BY RICHARD HAPPER

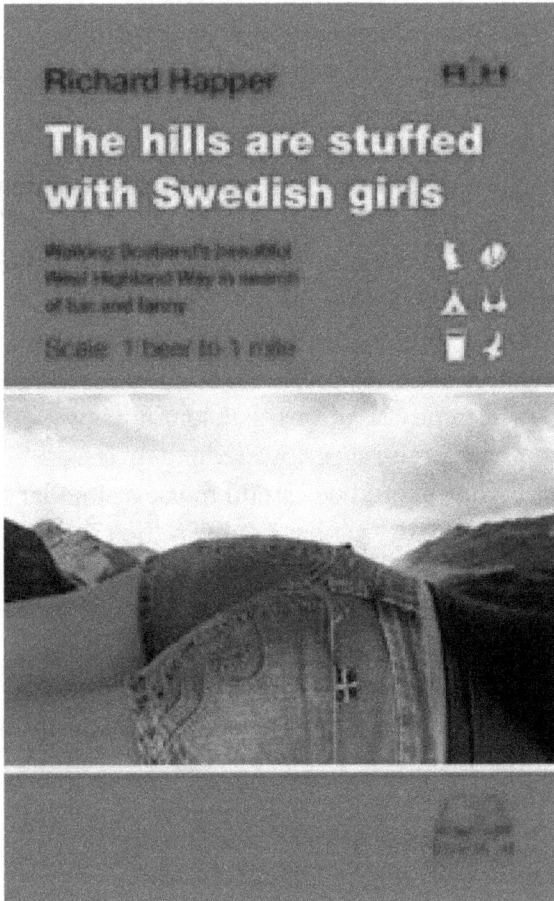

Join three lovesick men on a mission through the beautiful highlands of Scotland (with their cat) in search of the elusive and mythically gorgeous Scandinavian tourist girls. An amusing and very touching novel by Richard Happer.

You can get in touch with Richard on LinkedIn or Twitter @richardhapper